Text copyright © 1992 Norman Warren
Cover illustration copyright © 1999 David Salmon
This edition copyright © 1999 Lion Publishing

The author asserts the moral right
to be identified as the author of this work

Published by
Lion Publishing plc
Sandy Lane West, Oxford, England
www.lion-publishing.co.uk
ISBN 0 7459 4132 X

First edition 1992
10 9 8 7 6 5 4 3 2 1

A catalogue record for this book is available
from the British Library

Typeset in 12/13 Venetian 301
Printed and bound in Singapore

Why Believe?

Answers to key questions about the Christian faith

NORMAN WARREN

A LION BOOK

Contents

Who needs God?

'Why do I need to believe in God? The stars tell me all I need to know.'

'I believe in Mother Earth. She is my God.'

'I am the boss of my life. I don't need God.'

'I would like to believe in God, but look at the mess the world's in!'

'Is it really possible to know God?'

Most people today believe in something, someone, greater than themselves. Many would like to believe in God but find it so hard. To them, God seems far off, unconcerned with our daily lives with all their ups and downs.

For 2,000 years Christians have claimed that they know God through Jesus Christ, that it is possible to trust in him for time and eternity.

What does it means to have faith? Who is God? What is God like? Who is Jesus? Who is the Holy Spirit?

These are some of the questions we shall be looking at, so that you may discover what it means to have a living faith in God the Father, Son and Holy Spirit.

What is faith?

'I wish I had a faith like yours. How can I find faith?'

We show faith every day of our lives.

Every time we go on a train or a plane we are showing trust in the driver or pilot and in the engineers and the makers. We do not go up to the pilot and ask to see his licence every time we fly. We trust in him and in his ability. Nor do we have to understand how things work before we trust them. We probably have no knowledge of electricity, but we exercise faith every time we switch a light on. We may not know how a car works, but we trust it will go when we turn on the ignition.

We trust people all the time; life would be impossible unless we did and nothing would ever get done. We rely on people to help us, most of whom we never meet — people who supply us with food, power, money, services...

The focal point of faith is not so much what is in me, but rather in what, or whom, I am trusting. I may be nervous going up in a plane but I am trusting my life to the pilot. I will probably never meet him or see him, but I trust in him nevertheless.

A Christian is someone who trusts in God, who believes he is there, totally reliable and in full control.

An elderly lady was noted for her great faith in God.

'What is the secret of your faith?' she was once asked.

'I am a woman of little faith in a great God,' she replied.

To go back to our original illustration. You want to travel to another city. You go to the station, there stands the train. The porter assures you it is the right train. But simply believing it goes to your city will never get you there; you have to get on it and go!

Believing in God, knowing that he is there, is one thing. Committing yourself to him is another, and that is when faith springs into life.

Why believe in God?

'Who is this God that Christians believe in? What is he like? What does faith in God really mean?'

God is the name given to the creator of life. We either believe in a Creator God or we have to believe everything happens by chance. We cannot prove there is a God by reason or logic or argument. But then, you cannot prove love in this way either, but that does not mean love does not exist!

The amazing solar system and the world in which we live demands a master designer, an architect, an engineer and an artist. *We call this great being God.*

We human beings live in time and we have a beginning and an end. Just because we are like this we tend to think God must be the same. But the Bible tells us that God has no beginning and no end. He is not subject to time as we are.

Space, to all intents and purposes, has no beginning and no end; it stretches on and on. We find this hard to take in because our minds are limited. We can only understand what we can see and know and we think that must be everything. God is far greater than our minds can take in. He has always been there. He never changes or grows old as we do. God is the one unchanging factor in an everchanging world.

The world God has made is one of outstanding beauty and order. The whole world of nature shows clear signs of careful design and natural laws. We plant a daffodil bulb and up comes a daffodil. From a tiny egg in a woman's body there develops a child with all the intricate mechanism of ear and eye, mind and heart. But no parent can give life to that child. It is God who gives life – that strange, intangible mystery which defies analysis and which no one but God can create.

We cannot see God, though all around us are the signs of his handiwork. But there are many things in everyday life we cannot see – wind, electricity, air, radio waves – yet we know they are there. We cannot see love, yet we know it is there in those who care for us. We cannot see God with our eyes, but we know deep within us he is there.

God does not have a human body like ours. This does not means he does not have personality. God can think, love, plan, design and create. He has all the traits of personality, but without a single weak point or fault.

Jesus said, 'God is Spirit' – full of active energy and life with no limits in time or space. We too have a spirit, or soul. It is our personality, what we are deep down, the source of all our ideals and hopes and thoughts. God is all this to perfection. It is no wonder that Jesus went on to say that it is this great Creator God, Father of all, whom we are to worship in spirit and in truth.

How can I know God?

'Can anyone by searching find God? I long to know where I can find him!'

Modern ideas? They were written about 3,000 years ago. Every tribe and race since the beginning of time has tried to find God. There is something, deep down in all of us, that is searching for God, whether we acknowledge it or not. All the great religions of the world are part of that search.

If we are to discover more about God we cannot do it on our own. God has to make the moves towards us. He has to reveal himself more clearly than just through the created world.

In the past God made his will known through holy men and women who lived close to him. He gave moral laws, the Ten Commandments, to Moses for the Hebrew people and, indeed, for all people for all time. If these laws were kept the world would be a far happier place: no stealing, no killing, no greed.

But the great and final revealing of God came in the person of Jesus. Everything else, everyone else, are hazy shadows. As we look at Jesus, we see God in person. One of Jesus' followers, Philip, made this request of Jesus:

Show us the Father. That is all we need!

Jesus replied,

Anyone who has seen me has seen the Father.

In his Gospel account of Jesus' life, John is careful to show that Jesus did not come into existence at Bethlehem. That was the way he chose to enter our world. But he has always existed:

He was with God and he was the same as God.
From the very beginning he was with God.
Through him God made all things; he was the source of life.
He became a human being and, full of grace and truth, lived among us and we saw his glory, the glory which he received as the Father's only son.

Why believe in Jesus Christ?

❛Who was Jesus? Just a man? Or was he God?❜

Jesus is the one way to God: fully human and yet fully divine. Perfect man and perfect God.

He was fully human, born of the Virgin Mary. He grew up in an ordinary family and spent the early years of his life working as a carpenter in the small Galilean village of Nazareth.

At about the age of thirty he left home and travelled around for just three years, teaching, healing and caring for all in need. On several occasions he raised the dead to life in full view of witnesses. He ordered evil spirits to leave those who were possessed, bringing peace and wholeness to their minds.

His wonderful and unique teaching about the kingdom of God, which no other teacher has ever begun to match, was backed up by a perfect life with no stain of sin or selfishness. He was at home with all people, accepting them and treating them with respect, no matter who they were or what they did.

Jesus knew what it was to be hungry and thirsty and to be so tired that he fell asleep in a small boat in the middle of a storm. He knew what it was to weep in deep personal grief and he experienced loneliness and desertion by his friends. He went through the most excruciating pain when he was mercilessly flogged and crucified – the most painful death the ancient world could devise – but even the Roman Governor admitted he could find no fault in him. Jesus was a perfect man in every way.

But alongside his perfect life and marvellous teaching, Jesus made the most astonishing claims:

▌'The Father and I are one,' he once said, claiming equality with God.

▌He said he was able to forgive sins, claiming openly to do what only God can do.

▌He said that he was the only way to God: 'I am the way, the truth and the life. No one comes to the Father except by me.'

▌He promised peace to all who came to him: 'Come to me, all of you who are tired from carrying heavy loads, and I will give you rest.'

▌He claimed that he would raise to eternal life all who trust in him: 'My sheep listen to my voice; I know them and they follow me. I give them eternal life, and they shall never die. No one can snatch them away from me.'

To know him is to know God.
To trust him is to trust God.
To honour him is to honour God.

Jesus was either a fraud, or badly mistaken, or just plain mad – or else he was what he claimed to be. This was what one of his followers, Thomas, discovered. At first he refused to believe that Jesus had risen from the dead, but then he met the risen Christ face to face and fell at his feet in love and worship: 'My Lord and my God.'

Why did Jesus die?

'What happened when Jesus died on the cross? Can one person's death affect me today?'

Jesus came to show us what God is like. He did this by his life and teaching. He described God's love and truth and justice, usually in vivid, everyday stories that anyone could understand. But his main reason for coming was to deal with the root problem in every living person: pride and self-centredness. This is what is wrong with the world. This is the cause of all quarrels and all breakdown in relations between individuals and nations… 'I want my way!' 'Me first!' The Bible simply calls this sin.

So sin is not just killing, stealing and doing wrong things. It is deep-rooted in the whole of humanity. Sadly, we live in an imperfect world, full of pain and suffering, rejection and anger. We are all part of this. What others do and say affects us and causes pain and hurt. Abuse of one kind or another in childhood – physical, mental or sexual – can damage a person in later life through no fault of their own and can make them feel of little or no value.

The egotism of a Hitler or Stalin, the greed of the drug barons, cause untold suffering to huge numbers of people. Human sin breaks down relations between people and it also breaks down relations with God so that he seems to be remote and unconcerned about our world and our life.

There is no way we can get back to God; we are simply not good enough! What was needed to change this situation was someone with no personal sin or wrong, someone perfect in every way, who could bring us back to God.

Before this could happen, the problem of human sin had to be dealt with. God dealt with it in a remarkable way.

God is not only perfect love; he is also perfect justice. His justice rightly demands that all sin and wrong must be punished. We all recognize that a judge must uphold the law and justice must be done, otherwise anarchy will reign everywhere. But God's perfect love is also shown, by sending Jesus into our world to take in his own sinless self all our sin and guilt. If there had been any other way, then God would certainly have found it.

Jesus suffered on the cross the death penalty our sins rightly deserve. Because the consequences of our sins were laid on him, he experienced the hell of being cut off from his Father as he hung there on the cross.

My God, my God! Why have you forsaken me?

On the cross Jesus took on himself all the effects of human sin; all the feelings of isolation and abandonment, all the pain and suffering, all the rejection and anger of the whole of humanity.

Just before he died, Jesus cried out, 'It is finished!' His work of saving us from sin and death and hell was complete. These words can also mean that a debt is paid.

The huge debt of human sin was paid once and for all. The way back to God and to full forgiveness is wide open. The bridge has been reopened between God and us. Friendship with God is there for all who come to Jesus in love and trust. One of those watching by the cross was Peter, who later wrote:

> *Christ himself carried our sins in his body on the cross. Christ died for sins once and for all, a good man on behalf of sinners, in order to lead you to God.*

This lovely and well-known hymn puts it so simply and so clearly:

> *He died that we might be forgiven,*
> *he died to make us good,*
> *that we might go at last to heaven,*
> *saved by his precious blood.*

Why believe he rose again?

‘What happened after Jesus died? Did he really come back to life?’

There was no doubt about it: Jesus was dead. As dead as a doornail. The Roman soldiers made sure of that. Nor was there any doubt that Jesus was buried. Joseph of Arimathea took the dead body of Jesus and had it put in the tomb which he had presumably reserved for himself. A huge stone was rolled over the entrance and Roman soldiers were posted to guard it.

All Jesus' friends knew that he was dead too. There was no doubt about it; they had watched him die. They had seen him buried, and for them that was the end of everything. All their hopes were sealed in that tomb.

But on the first Easter day, when women came to the tomb in the hope of anointing Jesus' body, they found the stone rolled back, the body gone and the tomb empty except for the grave clothes. These were still there, wrapped as though the body had just gone clean through them. But who had moved that stone and what had happened to the body of Jesus?

The Jews and the Romans certainly did not take it, otherwise they would have produced the body when the disciples claimed that Jesus had risen from the dead. The friends of Jesus did not take it; they knew the tomb was guarded and they were a group of disillusioned and totally broken people. In any case, they certainly would not have risked their lives later in proclaiming what they knew to be a lie.

There is no other explanation for what has been called 'the most proven fact of history'. Jesus rose again on the third day after his death. Nothing else can possibly explain the empty tomb and all the appearances of Jesus, sometimes to one person, then to a couple on the open road, then to the disciples, then to crowds of people — sometimes in a room, sometimes by the sea or on a hill and in broad daylight.

Jesus met them, talked with them and they could touch him. He was the same Jesus, yet somehow different. Now he was no longer subject to time and space. You can read it in Luke chapter 24 and John chapters 20 and 21.

Nothing else can possibly explain the total change in the disciples. They were a small, frightened group huddling together behind closed doors. But now they became people full of joy and courage, going out into the market places of the world fearlessly proclaiming that Jesus had risen from the dead. Now they knew beyond any shadow of doubt that Jesus was far from being an ordinary man. He was truly God!

'Jesus is Lord' was their message. Lord of heaven and earth, Lord of all people and nations, Lord of time and eternity, Lord of our lives, Lord of all. So the apostle Paul could write:

In honour of the name of Jesus, all beings in heaven and on earth and in the world below will fall on their knees and will openly proclaim that Jesus is Lord, to the glory of God the Father.

Why believe Jesus ascended into heaven?

'Where is Jesus now? What authority does he have in the world?'

Jesus had come from heaven to earth.

He had completed the work he had to do. Now it was time to return home and, for Jesus, heaven was home.

While on earth Jesus limited himself to being in only one place at a time, he promised he would send the Holy Spirit to be with every Christian everywhere. In this way, the work he had started could be carried on through the lives of his people. His followers needed to live without his physical presence.

The ascension, when Jesus returned to God's closest presence, was the final proof of his victory over sin and death. It showed beyond any shadow of doubt that his sacrifice on the cross for our sins was perfect; once and for all, never to be repeated. It also marked the beginning of Jesus' heavenly work. As he said before he finally left his disciples:

I have been given all authority in heaven and on earth.

Christian creeds speaks of Jesus 'seated at the right hand of God'. This is simply a picture of his total authority over all creation. The world and the universe are under his control, and slowly and surely his will for the whole of creation is being worked out. We may not always be able to see it and we may wonder at times why certain things happen, but nothing can prevent his purpose being done in history and in the world, in his way and in his time.

There in heaven is the Lord Jesus Christ, our representative right in the very presence of God. He is our guarantee that we are God's people, that we belong to him and his kingdom and that we will be with him for ever.

Because he became man, he fully understands us and all that we go through.

Because he is God, he has all power and love to help us.

The knowledge that Jesus is Lord of all brings inner peace and a deeper faith. We know he is in full control, not only of the world, but of all our lives as well. Nothing can ever take us from his presence:

I am with you always, to the end of the age.

It gives Christians the confidence and courage to be witnesses to Jesus. For he promises the inner power to tell what we know of him.

It brings the certain hope that we have a home in heaven when we die, which Jesus is preparing for us:

There are many rooms in my Father's house, and I am going to prepare a place for you so that you will be where I am.

What is baptism?

‘Why are people baptized? Does it make us Christians?’

The word 'baptism' comes from a Greek word that means to dip or plunge, or even to cleanse by washing. It was used of someone deep in debt or plunged into sorrow, of a ship sinking into the sea or of washing clothes in water.

The Hebrew people used a kind of baptism about a hundred years before Christ, for non-Jews who wanted to become Jews. Then John the Baptist came onto the scene. He challenged the Jews to turn from their selfish ways and seek God's forgiveness. To show they really had repented and that simply being sorry was not enough, he called them to be baptized in the River Jordan.

Jesus himself came to John to be baptized. He wanted to show, publicly, his total obedience to his Father's will. For Jesus, baptism was an act of complete commitment and dedication.

The followers of Jesus baptized those who not only repented but who also turned to Jesus in faith and obedience. Baptism became the mark, or symbol, of entry into the Christian faith. Those who turned to Christ were baptized in the name of the Lord Jesus Christ, to show their oneness with him.

To begin to understand the full meaning of baptism, we need to go right back to the Old Testament, to the story of Abraham. God was looking for people to love him and follow his laws. He found in Abraham a man who was willing to do this. God promised to make of him a great nation and to bless him. To mark this agreement, or covenant, God ordered Abraham to be circumcised and to circumcise every baby boy, as an outward sign that he belonged to the people of God.

The sign of God's covenant with his people, all down the years until the coming of Jesus, was circumcision. But now the kingdom of God is open to people of all races and nations, not just Jews. The sign of the new people of God is now baptism, not circumcision.

Whether baptism is offered to adults or to infants, its meaning is the same. The Bible gives us several helpful pictures to bring out this meaning. Going into the waters of baptism is like dying to the old way of life, finishing once and for all with the life of 'self' first, and determining to live for Jesus.

On a Greek island an old Christian chapel was discovered which had a font shaped like a huge cross. Early on Easter morning those to be baptized would stand at one end of this font, which was filled with water. They would profess their faith in Jesus and then go into the water as if into the cross, and in a memorable way demonstrate their oneness with Jesus' death. They would come up the other side as if risen with Christ – one with his resurrection and victorious life!

Water is used in baptism to describe washing from sin.

Just as water washes our bodies clean, so baptism is a vivid symbol of the cleansing of the human heart from the stain and dirt of sin.

Baptism also marks a person's entry into God's family. The birth of a baby is a family occasion – a new child for a human family. The baptism of a person is a church family occasion and marks the entry into God's family.

We are not members of God's family automatically, just by being born. You have to be born into it in a spiritual sense. Not by doing things, even good and religious things, but through God, by his mercy, bringing us into his family through faith in Jesus. Baptism is the sign of this new birth. It marks the beginning of a new life that will go on and on as we grow more like Jesus.

In one way baptism is an individual thing: I turn from my self-centred way of life, and trust in Jesus. But baptism is far more than this. By baptism you are made one with Jesus and also with his body, the church. Paul, in a marvellous passage, describes the church as the body of Christ and each Christian as a vitally important member:

In the same way all of us have been baptized into the one body by the Holy Spirit.

Baptism is also signing on in God's army, a commissioning to go to war! In many churches, when someone is baptized, they are signed on the forehead with the cross with words such as these:

Fight valiantly under the banner of Christ against sin, the world and the devil, and continue Christ's faithful soldier and servant to the end of your life.

The Christian's life is not a pleasure cruiser, sailing smoothly on calm, sunlit seas. It is a warship, crashing through heavy waves with the enemy all around!

Christians have in Jesus the most wonderful friend of all. Though the devil is a powerful and implacable enemy, they serve a leader who cannot lose, for Jesus won the victory over the devil on the cross and we share in that victory.

What a vivid picture is baptism. It tells us of new life, of cleansing, and of being members of a great army, victorious for Christ.

Why believe in the Holy Spirit?

'Who is the Holy Spirit? How can he change our lives?'

Each one of us is a kind of trinity – a three-in-one. We are body, mind and spirit, yet we are one being. And God too is revealed as a Trinity: one God, yet three distinct persons: the Father, the Son and the Holy Spirit. All are equal; all are God.

The Holy Spirit is not some vague influence or ghostlike creature. He is a person in every way, yet without the human body we have. He has a mind and a will. He can love, guide and help. He possesses all the power and authority of God, for he is God every bit as much as the Father and the Son. He is all-powerful, all-knowing and present everywhere.

The Holy Spirit's work is to help people to trust in Jesus. He it is who makes us realize our need of him and his forgiveness. He it is who comes to live within us when we open our hearts to Jesus. He is the promised gift to every Christian, bringing that calm confidence that we are children of God.

It is the Holy Spirit, working in our lives, who helps us to grow more like Jesus every day. He can produce in our lives, often without our realizing it, the lovely fruit that should be the mark of every Christian.

The Spirit produces love, joy, peace, patience, kindness,
goodness, faithfulness, humility and self-control.

The Holy Spirit will help us to overcome temptation and bad habits. Even though the Holy Spirit lives in us, we still have our old natures that will be with us until we die, trying to pull us back to old ways of living. The Holy Spirit is there to help you resist this downward pull and grow strong in faith.

Only the Holy Spirit can change human nature and make a self-centred person more like Jesus. Only the Holy Spirit can turn that anger and bitterness into forgiveness and acceptance. It is the Holy Spirit who helps us to pray and understand the Bible. It is the Holy Spirit who is there to guide us in those difficult decisions of life and lead us to discover God's will. He enables us to develop the gifts God has given us to serve him in the world.

The Holy Spirit is Jesus' gift to every Christian to prepare us for that day when we meet him face to face. As Paul's letter to the Romans assures us:

God has poured out his love into our hearts by means
of the Holy Spirit, who is God's gift to us.

Why believe in the church?

'Is the church really important? Are Christians better together than separate?'

Christians are people who have put their trust in Jesus Christ. They have been born again into God's family. Just as by the human processes of birth you were born into a human family, so, by the work of the Holy Spirit in you, you are born into God's family. The sign or mark of entry into God's family is baptism. Another name for God's family is the church.

The church is not bricks and mortar and glass; that is what a church building is made of. The church is people, people who belong to Christ; a great family in which all are brothers and sisters, from the greatest to the least, bound not by flesh and blood but by the Holy Spirit. There is no inequality; no one is more important than anyone else. All are equal in God's sight. The church consists of people who have been chosen by God, even before the world began – to be his children, to live pure and loving lives.

Even before the world was made, God had already chosen us to be his, through our union with Christ, so that we would be holy and without fault before him.

The church is not a sect or denomination, Catholic

or Protestant. It is a worldwide body of people, drawn from all colours, races and backgrounds, young and old; all who trust and follow Jesus Christ.

The church is also described in the Bible as a 'body' – Christ's body – with him as the head. Each believer is a member of that body, with his or her own gift or contribution to make to its proper working. Paul describes this in great detail in his first letter to the Corinthians, chapter 12, verses 12 to 31. God wants everyone in the church to use their gifts to build up the body in love and service.

The church is also God's people, citizens of his kingdom, called out of the darkness of unbelief into the light and truth of Christ.

The purpose of the church is to worship God, to make known to everyone God's love and to make disciples of all nations. It is to be his special witness in the world.

Jesus is the Lord of the church and it is he whom the church loves, worships and obeys. Nothing is more important in the life of the Christian than meeting together to worship him week by week. It is not just a duty but should be a delight to meet with other Christians.

In this way we show our love for him and for each other. As the Bible is read and taught, so we will grow in our faith. As we pray together, those we pray for will be helped and healed. It marks us out as followers of Jesus.

The church is like an army, God's army, engaged in a

deadly battle against human and spiritual wickedness. Jesus himself promised that even the gates of hell cannot stand against the church of Christ. It is a battle to be fought with the weapons of prayer and truth, purity and love.

The church may seem weak in the light of the tremendous forces of evil, but we live in God's world and Jesus is in control, ruling supreme over all. So final victory is certain.

Why the Lord's Supper?

'What happens at a communion service? How does it help our faith?'

Some people call it the 'Eucharist', which comes from the Greek word 'thanksgiving'. We thank God for all his gifts to us, especially the death of Jesus on our behalf, and we remember how he gave thanks as he took the cup of wine at the Last Supper.

Some people call it the Holy Communion, which stresses our unity with Jesus Christ and with each other. Some call it the Mass, which comes from the end of the service in Latin, from the word which means 'to dismiss'. We are sent out from worship to be Jesus' witnesses to the world. Others call it the Breaking of Bread, with the emphasis on the action of Jesus at the Last Supper.

It is often called a 'sacrament', from a Latin word meaning 'oath' or 'pledge'. It was used for the oath a Roman soldier made when signing on in the Emperor's army. In the outward physical symbols of the bread and wine, God promises to his people an inward blessing, and we pledge our love and obedience to him.

Each of these titles tells something more about this wonderful act of worship given to us by Jesus himself.

It all began about 3,000 years ago in Egypt. The Hebrew people had been slaves there for centuries, when

God sent Moses to set them free. Nothing would make the King of Egypt let them go until God passed a final judgment on the nation. All their first-born sons would die, and only those who smeared the door posts with the blood of a lamb would be saved. The Hebrew people did this, and then each family feasted on the lamb before they set out on their flight from Egypt. In memory of this they continued to celebrate their amazing deliverance with a Passover Supper each year.

It was this that Jesus was celebrating with his followers on the last Thursday evening of his life. He gave it a new meaning. His people would be saved not from physical slavery but from sin and eternal death. He would be the Lamb; his body would be broken in death and his blood poured out in sacrifice. So he took bread and broke it:

This is my body, which is given for you.

Then he took a cup of wine:

This is my blood, poured out for you.

For Christians, right down the centuries, this has been the most precious of all acts of worship. As we gather round the Lord's table, the presiding minister takes the bread and wine. It is to remind us in a vivid, visual way of his death for us. The president takes the bread, using the same words as Jesus used, and gives it to the people, and then takes the cup, repeats the words that Jesus used and shares it too with the people. The apostle Paul tells us we are to do this until Jesus comes again, when such a memorial meal will no longer be necessary.

In a manner that defies analysis, Jesus comes to his people, and as we take the bread and drink the wine we are demonstrating our oneness with him. He promises to be right there in the centre of his people. We come as his body, his family, his children, to be strengthened in our faith and witness.

This service is so important that Paul tells us we should prepare ourselves very carefully before we come. We are to come in openness to God, aware he knows all about us and that we can hide nothing from him. We are to come in humility, with open hands, to receive from him the Bread of Life. We do not presume to come to him trusting in our own goodness but in true repentance, aware of the wrong things we have done in word, thought and action, and also of the good things we have not done through carelessness, thoughtlessness or selfishness.

We are to come believing that he will accept us, forgive us, cleanse us and strengthen us by his Spirit to live for him in our daily lives.

Why believe in the Bible?

'**What sort of book is the Bible? What does it mean to call it 'inspired'?**'

The Bible is a library. The word comes from the Greek *biblia*, which means 'books', for it is a collection of books, sixty-six in all, divided into two sections. The first section is the Old Testament; this tells the history of the Hebrew nation before the time of Jesus' coming. It is also the Jewish Bible. The second is the New Testament and this tells of the life, death and rising again of Jesus. It then goes on to describe the way the Christian church grew, and contains the many letters to the churches which give clear instruction on how to live the Christian life in a secular society.

The Bible took over 1,500 years to be completed, so most of the writers never met and, in many cases, did not know what the others had written. Yet there is an amazing unity and agreement, and a common theme running through all the books: of God making himself known to humankind. He revealed his will to men and women who lived close to him. He guided them by his Holy Spirit to write down his words and instructions. This is why the Bible is often called 'the word of God'.

We can see the different personalities of the writers as they interpreted God's truth in their own way. So Peter said:

Holy men of God spoke as they were moved by the Holy Spirit.

Paul sums it up:

All scripture is inspired by God.

Jesus promised his followers that the Holy Spirit would remind them of all the things he had said and done:

*He will teach you everything and make you remember
all that I have told you.*

The Bible is so important to the Christian because it tells us what God is like in a way that nothing and no one else can. Without the Bible we would know very little about God and his plans. It speaks with clear authority on life and death and eternity. It is, indeed, a guide book for our journey through earth to heaven.

It is packed full of history, yet it is more than just a history book. It has gripping stories and lovely poetry, but it is more than just literature. It gives penetrating insights into human nature and tells us much about our world, but it is far more than a book of philosophy. Its main purpose is to lead us to faith in Jesus Christ. The whole Bible revolves around him.

The Old Testament prepares the way for his coming and the New Testament concentrates on his life in detail. Martin Luther, a great German Christian of the sixteenth century, once said:

Just as we come to the cradle to see the baby, so we go to the Bible to see Jesus Christ.

If you have never read the Bible, don't start at the beginning and try to read it right through, because you will probably very soon get bogged down in the laws of Leviticus. Begin with the Gospels of Mark and Luke and then John. After that, read the Acts of the Apostles and Paul's letter to the Philippians. Ask your Christian friends which are their favourite psalms.

Come to the Bible humbly, because it is God's word, and different from all other books. Read it expecting God to speak to you in your situation. Pray for the Holy Spirit to open your mind to understand what you read and to give you the strength to apply it to your daily life.

The real way to put the Bible to the test is as we read it and then follow its teaching. Paul wrote these words to a young Christian leader, Timothy:

Remember that ever since you were a child you have known the Holy Scriptures, which are able to give you the wisdom that leads to salvation through faith in Christ Jesus. All scripture is inspired by God and is useful for teaching the truth, rebuking error, correcting faults and giving instruction for right living, so that the person who serves God may be fully qualified and equipped to do every kind of good deed.

Why believe in prayer?

'How can we pray? Does God hear our prayers?'

Prayer is both speaking and listening. In any friendship there needs to be both. The Christian life is a friendship with Jesus Christ, and prayer is one of the ways this friendship deepens.

Prayer for the Christian is what air is for the human body. It should be as natural as breathing. It is speaking with Jesus about anything, anywhere and at any time. Prayer links us directly to him so that his help and guidance are available always.

Prayer is not just asking for things. It is also being consciously in his presence and sharing with him all that is going on in my life. Prayer can be either silent or spoken. It is true that God is almighty and all-knowing, but just as a parent loves to hear all that a child has been doing, so our heavenly Father delights to hear all our hopes and joys, fears and concerns.

Even Jesus, when on earth, prayed to his Father. If he felt he needed to, how much more do we, his followers? For him it was not only a duty but a delight, and so it should be for the Christian.

Prayer opens a channel between God and the one for whom we are praying. We do not need to tell God what to do, but simply to lay that person, in their special need, before him.

One of the loveliest illustrations of prayer is given to us in the story about four men who wanted to bring their paralyzed friend to Jesus. They could not get near him because of the crowd, so they climbed up onto the flat roof of the house where Jesus was and then lowered their friend through the opening, right at the feet of the Teacher! They did not tell Jesus what to do: they simply brought him to Jesus and placed him in his presence.

God always hears and answers our prayers, but in his own way and his own time. Sometimes the answer is 'yes', sometimes 'no' and sometimes 'wait'.

Prayer follows most naturally from reading the Bible, for there God speaks and we can know his will. Few things are more important than praying as God wants.

How, then, should we pray? There are no hard-and-fast rules, but the following suggestions may help:

▌*Be still*. Remember the one to whom you are coming. It may help you to meditate on a passage such as Psalm 95 or Psalm 100. Enjoy being quiet in God's presence and relaxing in his love for you.

▌*Say sorry*. We frequently need God's forgiveness, and it may well be right to ask him to forgive something you have said or done that is causing you and others concern and pain.

▌*Say thank you*. Spend a few moments remembering all

that you have for which to thank God. It is rare indeed that we cannot be thankful for something!

▌ *Pray for others*. It may well help to have a list of people to pray for: family and friends, church and state leaders. Use your imagination as you pray. Try and picture the person and their special situation. Pray as you watch the news and read the newspaper.

▌ *Pray for yourself*. Pray about every aspect of your life. Be open with God, and share with him your fears and hopes and plans.

▌ *Pray with other Christians*. There is a special joy in meeting with other Christians in a group to pray. Jesus gives a clear promise about answering prayers when two or three meet in his name. Pray constantly. You do not have to close your eyes to pray; you can pray at any time – the lines are always open!

Live a life of prayer in constant touch with Jesus, your Lord and Friend.

Why believe in life after death?

'What will happen to us when we die? Is there a life beyond?'

Death seems so final.

A body, once vibrating with life, now is deathly pale and still. As we watch it lowered into the grave or disappear from sight at the crematorium, can we really believe that there is life after death?

Human beings have always believed in something. From earliest times, weapons, tools, even food, were put into the grave with a dead person, to help them on their journey to the next life.

But the fear still remains; life beyond the grave seems so vague and uncertain. The cry has always been, 'If only someone could come back from the dead and tell us!'

Someone has done just that... Jesus Christ! He alone can speak with authority on life after death. He came from heaven to earth, entering our world. He went through all the experiences of life, even death. But death could not hold him; he conquered it and rose victorious. He knows the eternal world beyond our world, and so he can speak from experience and with calm certainty.

Jesus speaks of two eternal worlds, heaven and hell.

Hell is where God has withdrawn his presence and his love. Jesus describes it as a place of darkness, weeping and torment. God sends no one to hell, but people will go there of their own choice if they ignore or reject the one way of forgiveness.

If a doctor prescribes a life-saving medicine and a person refuses it, it is certainly not the doctor's fault if that person dies. God has prescribed the answer to our deepest problems, and we turn our backs on Jesus at our eternal peril:

Salvation is to be found through him alone. In all the world there is no one else whom God has given who can save us.

Jesus describes heaven as home, the home of all God's people. Life here on earth is very short and time flies by. The Bible's message is that we do not belong here; we are like pilgrims passing through this world. For the Christian, our real home and country is heaven.

Jesus is preparing this for us. He will be there, with God the Father and the Holy Spirit. All who have loved and served him from the beginning of time will be there.

The Bible picture of heaven is of a place of perfect love and joy and peace. Words cannot even begin to describe it. It will be a new dimension of living, with no death, no evil, no violence or crime, no grief, no pain or suffering.

Jesus promises to raise our mortal body and give us a new body, as the apostle Paul describes in the fifteenth chapter of his first letter to the Corinthians.

Just as a bird has a body for flying in the air and a fish a body for living in the sea, so God will give us a body just right for living with him in heaven. There will be some link between our human body and this new body, just as there is a link between a bulb planted in the ground and the flower that springs from it. Yet one is so much more lovely than the other. Paul closes this chapter with the glorious words:

> *We shall be changed, the mortal changed into the immortal.*
> *Thanks be to God, who gives us the victory.*

All the puzzles of life will be solved and all the mysteries cleared up.

Those who love Jesus and trust in him need have no fear of death. When our body dies, as some day it surely will, the real person – our spirit, our soul, our personality – will go straight to be with Jesus. It will be just like going to sleep and we will wake up to see him and to live with him for ever.

> *Eye has not seen nor ear heard the things that God has*
> *prepared for them that love him.*

> *We are citizens of heaven and we eagerly wait for our*
> *Saviour, the Lord Jesus Christ, to come from heaven.*
> *He will change our weak mortal bodies and make them*
> *like his own glorious body, using that power by which*
> *he is able to bring all things under his rule.*

Why believe Jesus will come again?

'How will history end?'

This Jesus who was taken from you into heaven will come back in the same way as you saw him go into heaven.

These words were spoken to the followers of Jesus immediately after he had vanished from their sight and returned to be with God.

We have his promise on page after page of the Bible that he will come again. The first time, he came in great humility and quietness; only a few people were there to welcome him. He came to seek and to save the lost and it led to his suffering and death. But alongside this we have whole chapters that are devoted to the one theme, that Jesus will come again with great power and glory for all to see.

Jesus' second coming will mean the end of human history as we know it. He came the first time as Servant and Saviour; he will come the second time as Sovereign Lord of all.

What will his return be like?

Jesus tells us it will be sudden, like a thief in the night, when it is least expected; the world will be quite unprepared for it. It will be visible and open for everyone to see. It will not be quiet or secretive; the whole of creation will be fully aware of it. It will be glorious. Jesus will come in the clouds of heaven, with power. It will be final. This earth as we know it will have finished its purpose and will be destroyed, and there will be a new heaven and a new earth.

Peter describes this vividly:

> *The Day of the Lord will come like a thief. On that day the heavens will disappear with a shrill noise. The heavenly bodies will burn up and be destroyed and the earth with everything in it will vanish. But we wait for what God has promised, new heavens and a new earth where righteousness will be at home.*

The Jesus who comes then will be the same Jesus who came before, but it will be a day of judgment; those who know and love him will be separated for ever from those who have never acknowledged him as Lord.

Imagine a scene in a courtroom. The person brought before the judge is clearly guilty, and the judge must uphold the law. He does not hate the guilty person. He may feel very sympathetic and want to let the person go free, but he cannot do this because he must pass sentence.

Jesus will be the judge and his judgment will be absolutely fair. It will be passed on what each person has done in their lifetime with the light they have been given through Jesus. That decision will be the basis of what happens in eternity. Life as we know it will finish, but a glorious new life is there waiting for the children of God. For them there is no penalty to pay, because Jesus bore the penalty in his death.

When will this be?

The simple answer is that God alone knows! Jesus did tell us of signs that will herald his return: an increase in natural disasters, earthquakes and famines; wars and cruel, oppressive regimes, with Christians suffering fierce persecution. There will be an ever-increasing breakdown in relationships and growing fear and tension in the world. All kinds of false sects and religious leaders will arise, claiming to be God or to speak for God. The Good News of Jesus must be preached in every land.

All this is happening now, and increasingly so. All the signs are that Jesus' coming is getting very near.

The Bible constantly challenges us to be ready for Jesus at any time – either when we die or when he comes again. We should so live that nothing will make us ashamed should he suddenly come. We should be using our time wisely, and sharing the Good News of Jesus with others, that they too may come to know and love him.

Be on your guard, because you do not know what day your Lord will come.
Remain in union with Christ, so that when he appears we may be full of courage and need not hide in shame from him on the day he comes.